A STUDY SESSION *with* CHRIST

A STUDY SESSION *with* CHRIST

JEROME MCNEARY

A Study Session with Christ

Copyright © 2021 by Jerome McNeary. All rights reserved.

No part of this publication may be reproduced, stored in a retrieval system or transmitted in any way by any means, electronic, mechanical, photocopy, recording or otherwise without the prior permission of the author except as provided by USA copyright law.

The opinions expressed by the author are not necessarily those of URLink Print and Media.

1603 Capitol Ave., Suite 310 Cheyenne, Wyoming USA 82001
1-888-980-6523 | admin@urlinkpublishing.com

URLink Print and Media is committed to excellence in the publishing industry.

Book design copyright © 2021 by URLink Print and Media. All rights reserved.

Published in the United States of America

Library of Congress Control Number: 2021913775
ISBN 978-1-64753-880-4 (Paperback)
ISBN 978-1-64753-881-1 (Digital)

28.05.21

Synopsis

I had been studying God's word and taking notes for several years and one night while studying God came to me and told me to write this book. Check out how my study sessions turned into a full blown book. A vast majority of this book I myself have lived through and learned from experience. God truly works in mysterious ways. God was giving me knowledge in the middle of the night, I was getting out of bed to go and write. I also had to endure multiple attacks from the enemy, but through it all God kept me strong. I pray in the name of Jesus that it makes you stronger spiritually and brings you closer to God. Thank you and enjoy.

Bio

Jerome McNeary was born and raised in Tennessee. He began studying the word of God it was during one of these study sessions that he was led by the Holy Spirit to write a book on how to build a stronger relationship with God the Father. He currently resides in Memphis, Tennessee, with his wife, Deanna and their two small children.

Part 1

Obedience & Disobedience

Jeremiah 12:10-17

Obedience will always save you because it shows God that you trust him. And that's one of the things He really wants from us is trust; with trust comes knowledge and understanding of Him therefore bringing a closer connection with God.

Jeremiah 13

Disobedience, pride, and vanity highly angers God and brings upon His wrath, He knows all glory belongs to Him, and we ought to know and show the same thing. Pride also brings captivity, captivity humbles us and that's the state where God is most pleased with us, when we are humble.

Jeremiah 15

God grows angry with His people and is ready to destroy them. He says He "is weary with repenting", meaning God does get tired of hearing the "same old song" and will sooner or later turn a deaf ear to us and unleash His wrath on us for repetitive backsliding, all the begging and pleading in the world will not help. But there is good news, He also says "if ye return then I will bring thee again and thou shall stand before me". And also says, "I will make thee unto this people a fenced brazen wall: and they fight against thee but they shall prevail not". Also goes on to say that I am with thee. So as the Lord instructed me to say earlier obedience will always save you. But we have to treat our relationship with God like any other relationship. I mean you won't consistently offend or disrespect your spouse or significant other in fear of losing them, so God deserves the same or even better treatment. Now God understands that we are not perfect but he also understands that we are not ignorant, and we know better than some of the things we do. So He will not allow us to consistently hurt Him. God states in Jeremiah 17th chapter that blessed is the man who trusts in Him. Trust seems to be something that is drilled into our head throughout the bible. If we as humans can learn to trust God's voice on something as simple as making a right turn here while driving, not playing your favorite video game, watching your favorite TV show, or something of that nature we would see a much better quality of living. The voice of God is an "unfair advantage" in overcoming the world and having a prosperous life. If you consider that this is the voice of the one who created everything, controls everything, nothing gets past Him or happens without His approval. How could you not listen to His voice? Easier said than done right? Because usually God gives us an answer that we don't want to hear, this makes it hard to listen. That's why trust and obedience are so important especially when you put God's will before your own. Then it becomes a sacrifice. Paul writes in Romans 7:15 that he does the things he hates, earlier in that chapter he admits to being a carnal being and that he is sold under sin because of this. Therefore he does the things he hates his flesh) because he understands the two are at war (spirit and flesh). The flesh does not want to do the will of God. Therefore we should follow the spirit that is from God and wants to do His will. If you look at the leaders of the Old Testament such as Joshua and Moses you will see that they were victorious because they heard and listened to God not because they were supermen. Hearing, understanding, and listening to God's voice are the keys to victory.

Jeremiah 18

Sometimes God sees an example of what He is trying to tell us and will tell us to go there to see it. Perfect example, God tells Jeremiah to go to the Potter's House where he sees a parable of himself remolding the people of Israel. The vessels were marred and disfigured and the potter was restoring them just like he wanted to do with Israel, but the people were not listening to God, therefore provoking His anger. We must understand that God sees our life, our very existence as a war. Jesus said in Matthew 12:30, "he that is not with me is against me", also in Ephesians 6:12 says, we war not against flesh and blood. So when we turn our back on God He sees it as us going to the other side and there are consequences for that. When He was wroth with the people of Israel He said He would fight on the side of their enemies directly against them for they have turned their back on Him. But it's all to get your attention, God loves us more than we can imagine and His doors and arms are always open to us, but that does not mean run back and forth between God and the world. Because believe it or not God can get fed up just like us, one thing God has shown me is that basic relationship principles apply to His and our relationships. What God is trying to say is that we are just like Him remember we are made in His image and have a lot of His tendencies such as emotionally He hurts too, but if we can realize that He operates on a much higher level than we do we will see that the joy and pain He feels are much greater. I mean you would not want a person that you loved a great deal hurting you on a regular basis right? You would eventually get fed up and leave, but God says He will never forsake us, imagine wanting to leave but can't because of what you said. Very frustrating huh, that is the position we put God in a lot of the time. But the way to counter these actions is in His word if we simply listen to Him we will see the difference. Psalm 37:4 says delight yourself in the Lord and He will give you the desires of your heart. We serve a God that is ready to give us the world which is His anyway. If we delight ourselves in Him, this means our daily living should be in line with His word. From what we watch on TV to what we listen too. Have you ever heard the expression you are what you eat? The same thing applies in the spirit world; if you feed your spirit with ungodly things then your spirit will eventually be ungodly. When I say feed your spirit I mean things we allow into our heads that eventually leaks into our hearts. Where your heart is also is your spirit, meaning they are connected. That's why GOD says he speaks to your heart. Gives new meaning to the phrase follow your heart doesn't it? If we can get our hearts lined up with GOD'S will and be on one accord with him the possibilities are truly endless, everything Jesus promised us will be right there. I watched a documentary on voodoo and witchcraft. And they interviewed some people over in Africa who said they actually saw people flying. Now think on that, if the enemy can give his followers that type of power I know our GOD can, but our time to do such things has not arrived yet, remember Jesus said "greater works ye shall do". Jesus came as a "model" a prototype so to speak of what a Christian should be, and should use the life of Jesus as a measuring rod to keep us straight, now don't get me wrong there's only one Jesus, but we still can try to be as close to him as we can. That's all

GOD wants is for us to try, make a decision to love him, not because someone told you to but because of whom he is and what he's done. None of us would be in the position we're in if not for GOD and we should thank him for it whether good or bad. I say that cause of this, what looks like trouble to us is always good in GOD'S eyes because he knows the outcome; victory in him, we can't lose as long as we have a close relationship with him. Isaiah 54:17 is still true people and will always be. I pray that we as believers understand the power we have in Christ and utilize it. Jesus said in John 14:12 that "he that believeth in me, the works that I do shall he do also; and greater works than these shall he do; because I go on to my father. So look at all the things our Lord did and think we will do all he did and more. And I know it's true because I with my own eyes have seen a man resurrected from the dead. But the key is getting closer to GOD is to get an up close, personal, and intimate relationship with him. GOD wants to be involved in your everyday life. But a lot of us don't want him involved that much we want "a little space". We want "a little space" when we go out and party and mingle, or when we go gamble or whatever we do were we feel we can't take GOD. But one thing I've learned is this; it's not where you go but it's who you bring with you. The feelings we get from indulging in our own will can't compare to what GOD wants for us. I'll take Buddism for example the followers of Buddah meditate daily and make it a point to give Buddah time every single day of their lives not just Sunday. Why can't we as Christians read our bible while the praises of our GOD play in our home as a serenade to the Lord in a attempt to get him to come into our homes. I challenge you as believers to invite GOD into your homes and your everyday lives. We have to learn to trust and be devoted to him and he will do the same and more for us. There is so much power in sacrificing for GOD, why do you think they did it so much in Old Testament times? But now GOD doesn't want animal or blood sacrifices anymore he wants habitual and emotional sacrifices. Give up your pride and those bad habits you know GOD doesn't like and replace them with some ones that will bring you closer to the father. That is how we get to victorious living in Christ. In John the 15th chapter Jesus talks about the "true vine" and how he is the vine and we as believers are the branches that sprout from the vine and he also says the father is the gardener and he takes away every branch that doesn't bare fruit, and he prunes the ones that do so they can bring forth more fruit. So it is in our best interest to be victorious in Christ, but only through him can you do so. It is only when you're living according to his purpose and will for your life that you are connected and favored of GOD therefore making you protected and "more than a conqueror" as Paul wrote. Another thing GOD likes to see is us being good stewards. He likes to see us manage his property. Have you ever been watching TV and see someone who is already rich win even more money, and you say to yourself, "they know they don't need anymore money". That's because they are good stewards therefore GOD sees fit to give them more. Think about it, would you give something of yours to someone who wasn't going to take good care of it? Then why should GOD? Jesus speaks about this in the parable about the servants and the talents (money) the servant with the least amount of money was the worst steward therefore he was cast out and his talents taken and given to the servant who had the most talents because he was the best steward out of the group. You can read this parable in the 25th chapter of Matthew. One thing about Jesus if you look at him closely you'll see he is very authoritative in what he believed and what he says, this is because he knows who he is and who he belongs too. Jesus left us all power in heaven and in earth through him and it is up to us to use it. If we could grasp the concept that Jesus had that "all things that the father has are mine." (John 16:15) We would carry ourselves a whole lot differently than we do now. Paul wrote in Romans 8:29 "that whom he did foreknow, he also did predestinate to be conformed to the image of the son, that he might be the firstborn among many brethren," basically saying that he wants a body of believers in the image of his son Jesus. He is the prototype, if we study Jesus and the way he handled things and try to be as he was that would bring us closer to the father. Things such as the spiritual mindset that Jesus has, he knows that the flesh follows the spirit, therefore keeping his mind on the spiritual aspect of every situation. Transferring this mindset into ours would make us a lot stronger spiritually. We need to be in constant thinking about how our decisions affect our spirit and our relationship with GOD the father. I'm not saying we should spend every waking moment thinking about it. But we do need to be aware of the consequences a bad decision will have on our relationship with GOD. We also should be aware that we all have been saved for a purpose, because that's what it all boils down to. Did you do the will of your father? Jesus himself confirms this in Matthew 7:21. But let me say this, just because your doing the will of our father doesn't mean it's going to be peaches and cream, there will be some trouble you can expect trouble. "Then why do it if it's not going to save me from trouble?" Though it will not save you from all trouble it will give more than enough strength to go through the trouble, and that's difference between believers and nonbelievers we have the strength to endure when others don't. But there's a method to the madness. When we were in the Garden of Eden we violated the trust of GOD. So now we have to pass certain tests to prove that we can be trusted. So basically what I'm saying is this, the more GOD can trust you the more he can give you. I mean you wouldn't give your belongings to someone you didn't trust, or would you?

Swagger

What if I told you that you had the power to take whatever you needed in the name of Jesus? Listen to what Jesus says in Mark 16: 17-18. "And all these signs shall follow them that believe; In my name shall they cast out devils, they shall speak with new tongues, they shall take up serpents, and if they drink any deadly thing it shall not harm them, they shall lay hands on the sick and they shall recover. And Asaph writes in psalm 82, "Ye are gods; and the children of the most high. And Jesus himself also states the same thing in john 10:34. That sounds like we are invincible. So right now in the name of Jesus our Lord and savior I'm declaring you invincible to the enemy and his attacks. Its promises like these that ought to give us a huge confidence boost about ourselves. And also, will give us the upper hand when battling the enemy. If you know what and who's you are nobody can tell you different, that makes you dangerous to the enemy because he can't feed off of your fear if you don't have any. Which in turn will give you the keys to success, and when you share that knowledge you defeat him even more by empowering the people of GOD. The enemy wants to see us living in poverty and lack, but Jesus wants us to live victoriously. And dominate the world instead of being dominated. I read in a book that talked about demonstrating the defeat of satan. It talked about how things work if you act out of faith instead of fear. It goes on to talk about how acting out of fear gives satan power over you, to torment you and to make things seem worse than they really are. And acting out of faith obligates the father to act on your behalf. This is because when you act out of fear you are saying to GOD that the "problem" is bigger than he is, and in turn you show no faith in him, therefore he won't help you because you don't believe in him. But when you act out of faith you are declaring GOD the father bigger than your "problem" and therefore he is obligated to honor your faith in him. So what does this mean to us? It means we have to use our knowledge of GOD'S word to determine when the enemy is trying to attack our faith. Let me give you an example. The enemy will often tell you what you can't do, when God says you and Him are a majority; you know stuff like that. Self- pity and doubt are signs that you are under attack because God says we are more than conquerors. God loves to see us overcome overwhelming odds through Him because that is our purpose now. I say now because it wasn't always like this in the garden of Eden we were meant to live in paradise forever but we were tricked out of it and a war was waged against our Father. And this is how we fight the war. The book of revelation talks a lot about overcoming the world and how we will be blessed for it. That should be a hint. So the next time your faced with a situation or you are knocked down by the enemy, don't sit there and cry, fight through it. It's what your father wants you to do. We are soldiers in an army. We were made to jump hurdles and move mountains. As a believer you have total authority over Satan through Christ Jesus our Lord and Savior, and nothing can stop you but you. So you have to make the choice live victoriously in the Lord and glorify Him in the process.

Freedom

What is freedom? Would you say it is the ability to make your own decisions, or do what you want when you want? I would say both. Let me ask you another question. Will you be able to do those things living in sin? (I'll let you answer that one.) Sin is more than just a pleasure of the flesh it is a trap, a ball and chain. I've never known a sin that didn't come with baggage. How about you? We know the wages of sin is death if you have not accepted Christ as your Lord and Savior, but there is another price to pay also, your freedom. Paul writes in Romans the 6th chapter about not letting sin rule your mortal body because we will end up obeying our flesh and not God. He also talks about the choices we have between yielding ourselves to sin unto death, or obedience unto righteousness. Basically saying we have the choice to be bound or free. The 6th chapter of Romans is a powerful chapter dealing with this subject. But not only does the Father want us to be free spiritually, but in all walks of life. Paul writes in Romans that if the Holy Spirit dwells in you it will also quicken your mortal body, meaning your physical body will prosper with your spirit. Think about that if your spirit is free your body will be free. Free from stress, debt, health issues, whatever you can think of. Now don't think the enemy won't attack you to make you think that this isn't true. Or try to give you the illusion that you are having problems and life is harder than what it is. But nothing and I mean absolutely nothing is bigger or has more power than you and God. Because you and God are a majority in any situation, against any army, and anything other than that told to you is a lie straight from hell. But you have to really get this concept because your faith determines this. Another concept you have to understand is how sin works and how it holds you back and away from GOD. Sin is an addiction; Webster's dictionary defines the word addict as someone who gives themselves up to a strong habit; usually in the passive voice. Does that sound familiar? If we look at sin as an addiction instead of a bad choice or a mistake, then we would know how to treat it and eventually be cured. The addict that beats his or her addiction is the one who really wants it, the one who really wants to quit and sticks with the process is normally the one who gets cured. Meaning that you rarely see someone quit cold turkey, it's a gradual process. So don't get down and give up when you slip and make a mistake it's always rough especially in the beginning. If you stick with the process you will eventually kick the habit. You know what your addiction is and you know the best way to beat it is to not position yourself to relapse. If your vice is shopping stay away from malls and stores unless you necessarily have to go. Now some of you just asked yourself "how is shopping a sin?" Well if you take money you should be paying a bill with or tithing with and go shopping then that's wrong. The way to kill anything is not to feed it. If you don't feed your addiction it will eventually die. And usually when your addiction is at a strong point or you have a real strong urge that's its way of telling you it's hungry. You have two choices, either feed it and allow it to grow stronger, or you can decide to not feed it and resist temptation and weaken it. Think about when you are hungry and your stomach growls if you don't eventually eat you will get weaker and eventually die right?

Well this same principle applies to your addiction. Withstanding temptation is the key to being freed from your addiction, being free from sin. And sometimes temptation comes as a way for the enemy to steal a blessing on the way from GOD. Remember the enemy can see ahead just like the father can, so withstanding temptation has its rewards in more ways than one. Even in your thinking, it needs to be free also, free from doubt and negativity. Which are tools of the enemy? If we can realize when the enemy is trying to hold us back from the blessings of GOD we would be better off. Let me give you an example, let's say GOD gives you a vision of you starting your own business, the enemy will come immediately and tell you why you should wait or why it wouldn't work. Doubt over anything over any situation in your life that will prosper you and is in line with GOD'S will should be confirmation that it is the right decision to make, Now if the spirit tells you otherwise that's different, but doubt leading to fear and confusion is another thing because God is not the author of confusion and GOD also does not deal in fear, GOD is a lot of things but one thing he is not is unsure. GOD gave us power and a sound mind, meaning we should be sure about our lives and where our lives are headed. The enemy only wants to see you struggling, worried, and stressed out, don't let him win. GOD'S will for us is that we prosper and be free, free through his only begotten son Jesus the Christ.

Another thing GOD wants to see from us is service, as we all know obedience is better than sacrifice. Serving GOD shows the spirit of obedience, therefore gaining a higher level of favor with him. Look at Isaiah 54:17, we all know the "no weapon" part, but read further and you'll see that it says this is the heritage of the servants of the Lord. Now everyone has a relationship with GOD be it good or bad and GOD speaks to us all so your way of communicating will be different from others. But if you are obedient and listen you can't go wrong. You'll see GOD work like never before, and your spirit and joy will reach new levels in Christ. Also GOD wants our service to speak for us, in the 6th chapter of Matthew Jesus teaches that when you do your alms don't do it before men just to be seen. He later says to them to do them in secret and thy father which seeth in secret himself shall reward thee openly. Now for those of us who don't know what alms are, (because I didn't), it is when you give gifts to the poor. So you don't have to run around and broadcast what you do to help others or your title at church and how much service you do for the body of Christ, but let your living say it for you. Another key to freedom is forgiveness, forgiving someone can be a hard thing to do sometimes, but it's the best thing for you. Jesus speaks about this also in the 6th chapter of Matthew. He says if you forgive men in their trespasses your father will forgive you of your trespasses. I'm sure we all want forgiveness from the father right? And also when you forgive someone you free yourself from them, in a way they have power over you if you stay mad at them. You notice how easy it is for someone to upset you when you have a grudge against them? You are giving that person a certain authority over your happiness by doing so. But when you forgive them you let go of what was done to you, and you also let go of the anger and the pain associated with the situation. Now let's get this straight the bible says forgive not forget, I myself have not read to forget in bible, but I have read to forgive. But just because you forgive someone doesn't mean you have to trust them again, that's between you and your spirit, it's your choice. You may choose to forgive someone for cheating in a relationship or something of that nature but because you forgave them doesn't mean you have to stay there in that relationship and continue to trust that other person, that choice is yours to make. You have to decide whether or not, if that person is still trustworthy or not.

Another key to freedom is understanding fear. And also how fear works, earlier we talked about fear and how the enemy responds to it, and on the other side how GOD responds to our faith. Check this out, the Webster's dictionary defines fear as to be in awe; reverence, it also says again to be in awe of. So by acting out of fear you are giving reverence to and are in awe of your enemy, who is beneath you. This really is a slap in the face of our father. Because you are his child and you accept him as your GOD, he promises us his spirit. Which if you receive will dwell in you. So by acting out of fear you are declaring that the enemy is greater than you and also GOD'S spirit that is in you and that is never the case. Saints understand that the enemy is a defeated foe and all of your reverence belongs to GOD our father. I also believe that the enemy has a plan just like our father. You have to remember he was with GOD for a long time being one of the first angels, so he works in a similar manner but for a totally different purpose. When going through trials and tribulations remember not to act out of fear, because our GOD is very able to overcome any and I mean any circumstance. GOD also wants us to prosper and to live victoriously in him through Jesus. If the enemy is able to instill fear in you he pretty much has you under his control. Now the definition for the word instill reads as follows; to put in drop by drop, to put an idea etc. In Ephesians the 6th chapter Paul writes about the armor of GOD, and the helmet of salvation is what I'm going to talk about because it protects your head. It protects your head in a war, also from the tricks of the enemy. Know in your mind and heart that you are saved and that nothing or no one can stand up to our father. Romans 8:28 is still very true. Now look at the flip side of it and look at the definition of faith; unquestioning belief, complete trust and confidence, loyalty. Does GOD deserve these things from you after all he's done? Now the reason I'm talking so much about faith is because of this, we as Christians really need to get how important faith is in our relationship with GOD. The stronger the faith the more we are able to overcome in Christ. And the less fear we have the less the enemy can do with us. Jesus himself said if we had faith the size of a mustard seed we could move mountains, just think about if we had faith the size of mountains. We could move the world and that's the whole point of the gospel of Christ. We are supposed to be movers and shakers in the name of Christ to show the world his power and that he is real and indeed lives on. We are supposed to influence the world but our faith has to be strong enough to do so. Even Jesus himself did his works by faith. If you read in the 9th chapter of Matthew you'll read that Jesus put out all of the nonbelievers before he resurrected a little girl. Nonbelievers speaking doubt and negativity will make it hard for you to do GOD'S work, that's why we should watch who we surround ourselves with. Your faith is the single most important thing you'll have in your relationship with GOD, so you have to protect it at all times. Paul writes in the book of Hebrews that is impossible to please our father without faith: for whoever comes to him must believe that he is. And also says that GOD is a rewarder of those who diligently seek him.

And last but certainly not least GOD wants us to be free financially. Now the key to financial freedom is a lot simpler than people think. One key is being a good steward over what GOD has given you already. It shows GOD he can trust you plain and simple. Another key is not being selfish with your money. Think about how you can help people out with your money instead of holding on to it and only being focused on yourself. Now I am not saying give all your money away, but I am saying help people in need. A highly successful businessman once told me of how he started his own business and how one of his goals were to and I quote " to give away as much money as I can outside of him living his lifestyle." Now what that meant was that he set a certain salary for himself to live off and everything after that he basically gave away. His business grew by leaps and bounds and he is very very comfortable financially. But he is still giving away money and GOD is still pouring more and more into him because GOD can trust him to do the right thing with the money.

And the most important key to financial freedom is (drumroll) tithing. This is a very touchy subject in most churches but it's one that needs to be addressed because tithing can either free you financially or bind you financially. Let me explain. GOD says in Malachi 3:10-11 that the people have robbed him of tithes and offerings therefore they are cursed with a curse but also says "try me in this and see if don't open up the windows of heaven. And pour out a blessing that you won't have room to receive." And says, " I will rebuke the devourer for your sakes, so he will not destroy the fruit of your ground." So saints this tells us that GOD is serious about us tithing. Look at it this way how would you like it if your church closed because of lack of tithing? How would you grow spiritually how would we come together and worship GOD for all he has done? How? It's easy to say "I'll just find another church." but will another church feed you and grow you like the one you've been at? Will it really be the same? I doubt it. Tithing for us is an especially important thing for everyone involved. But we must be careful not to fall in love with money also. The bible says that the love of money is the root of all evil. Now I am not saying wanting money is wrong, but I am saying falling in love with it and having that love control your decisions is. Decision making is also a huge factor in being free financially as well, even with all things mention previously, none of it matters if we make bad decisions with our money. Falling in love with money and letting it control you will eventually corrupt you and destroy your soul. JESUS said that we cannot serve GOD and mammon, for those of us who don't know (because I didn't) mammon is an idol god of money, so if you're not careful you can lose focus of GOD and end up putting money in his place and end up serving and worshiping it instead of the one and only wise true GOD who deserves all the praise. So, we should view money as nothing more than a tool we use to get the things that we want or need. Or simply as a tool to bless people and spread the goodness of GOD. We should dedicate ourselves to glorifying the name of GOD not getting caught up in dollars and cents. If we stay true to our passion which is the will of GOD the dollars and cents will take care of themselves. And also, decision making, remember your decisions should be conducive of the goal that you are trying to accomplish.

Going Through

Peter writes in his first epistle that our faith is tried with fire, now think about that for a second. Fire is the harshest element on earth. Nothing can survive it, so for Peter to compare our trials and tribulations to fire says a lot about what we must endure as believers. But know that GOD only wants to mold us into the people that Jesus saved us to be. Have you ever seen the making of a samurai sword? When a swordsmith makes a sword, he puts a hunk of metal in a huge furnace until it's red hot. And then he pulls it out and three to four men with sledgehammers beat on it. He repeats this process until he gets the hunk of metal to the shape he wants, and then he'll stick it in a tub of water instantly cooling it. And then he sharpens it on a grinder, and last but not least he paints and decorates it, giving it a "soul" as they say. When he is finished, he has turned a huge useless piece of metal into a beautiful indestructible weapon. GOD does that with us to strengthen our faith. The trails and trouble we see are only molding useless sinful creatures into beautiful indestructible weapons for our father to use. But saints our faith and trust in GOD enables us to make it through the transformation, understanding that GOD loves us and only wants the best for us. It's like going to fight for the heavyweight championship of the world knowing that the fight is rigged.

With no doubt you will win the fight; what kind of confidence would you have knowing if you just go in there and hold on you would win at some point? What type of swagger would you have coming to the ring? I got news for you, that is the type of swagger you should have coming into every trail and challenge you encounter like the fight is rigged, because it is. I say these things out of experience. I've come through situations where it looked like I was going to be out on the street with nothing. But in my storm GOD revealed to me the purpose for storms and why he allows us to go through them. If you can praise GOD, love and believe him in a time of need, if we can keep our joy and faith intact through the storm, then you have proved yourself worthy of the blessings of GOD. GOD also has revealed to me the importance of keeping your joy in tact through a storm and not letting negative emotions overwhelm you and pull you down. Remember when we talked about fear earlier in the book and how it makes your situation worse, the same holds true with all negative emotions, worrying, depression, doubt all attracts satan and his demons. Now on the flip side of that positive emotions such as joy, love, and patience attracts GOD and his angels. This is a critical test in us moving up in Christ. Before GOD moves you up to another level, another season in him, he has to be sure we are ready for it first. I was watching a martial arts exhibition, a student fending off a number of adversaries at one time. I mean like five on one. And after the student defended himself for a set amount of time the teacher stopped the exhibition let the pupil sit and it was time for another pupil to do the same, those who passed the test got a higher grade of belt, meaning they moved up a level in their art. And at the end the teacher himself got out there and defended himself against twice as many adversaries as the students. That was to show them their goal to be able to walk and move like or even better than him. But keep in mind the teacher has taught the students everything they need to know to pass the test. It's the same thing with us, our master has taught and given us everything we need to past the test that is in front of us. We just have to remember it and apply it to the situations that come up against us, so we can move up a level. Now really think about it, where is the place where you really get close to GOD? Where is the place that you really see how much GOD loves you? At the end of a storm is where. At that moment in time you feel closer than any other because of the victory you've won.

You know that all of your prayers have been answered, and your praises have been heard and were not in vain. It's a totally natural feeling. But we must remember that GOD wants our praises whether we are going through or not, GOD is still GOD and deserves all the glory. And praise and glory are a couple of things that you can withhold or give to GOD. Praise and worship to GOD are equivalent to a man and wife being intimate, it's a sign of affection, adoration towards GOD. The word praise is defined as to express approval or admiration of, also to glorify. And worship is defined as a service or rite showing reverence for a deity also intense love or admiration, title of honor used in addressing magistrates. I don't know about you, but I don't know of any magistrates higher than GOD. Just think of how GOD feels when we show these feelings towards him in the midst of a storm, when you think it's over you can still open your mouth and praise him, he has to honor that. Because that is a true sign of faith and belief in GOD, it also says to GOD, "I love you no matter what." And that's one of the main things this is all about anyway, the love between us and GOD. GOD just wants us to sincerely love him for him, not because of what he can do for us but for who he is and because he first loved us. Just like us, we want the same things in relationships.

So we should really understand where GOD is coming from on this matter. That's why praise is such a powerful weapon in your storm. It attracts GOD'S love and GOD'S love is stronger than any obstacle that can stand in your way. The bible says that GOD will inhabit the praises of his people. And where does your praise come from? It comes from inside of you and it goes out all around you. When you praise him you attract his presence. Assuming you have received his spirit. Now the Holy Spirit is vital in your relationship with GOD as far as being intimate goes. Because that is the only way he can dwell in you, that is the only way you and GOD can become one. The bible states that the spirit is a part of him. The reason I'm saying this is because of this saying, that "you plus GOD equals the majority." By you receiving the spirit, you and GOD are one making you the majority through GOD. That way you are the victor and not the victim. Another thing GOD has shown me is that he not only wants us to come out of situations he wants us to dominate the positions through our faith. GOD wants us to walk through the Red Sea and come out with dry feet or stand in a fire and come out with not so much as a scratch on us. The stories that I just referred to are just examples of what GOD wants to do for and through us.

Testimony

At this time, I was at my lowest point. I had just lost my job and was facing losing everything I worked so hard for. And at this point all the lies the enemy was telling me seemed true; stuff like GOD is upset with you, he's not going to save you this time, you're going to be forsaken, left on the street with nothing. The enemy was trying to get me to curse GOD and turn my back on him. And I did lose my home but didn't end up on the street. And after that didn't work, the suicide demons came. I found myself fighting off thoughts of suicide on a daily basis. Satan did not want to deal with what I was becoming in GOD so he tried to get me to kill myself; it's kind of funny when I look back on it. I found myself also being tormented by demons in the middle of the night. I can recall one incident when I heard a demon speaking to me in another language; it felt like I was getting the kitchen sink thrown at me. But GOD showed me in the midst of it all, that the enemy had no power over us as believers. It got to the point where I laughed at the demons that came to torment me in the middle of the night, they were nothing to me. GOD gave me strength in the middle of the hell I was going through. And I can say now I am much better because of the test GOD put in front of me. And you will be too if you believe that he is. Now let's get back to the book.

Enduring

But let me ask you this question. What happens when you've been praising GOD through the storm, speaking the word to your situations, giving all you have to stay faithful to GOD and you still see no change in your circumstance. What do you do then? Do you give up and quit? Meaning you stop believing GOD for his word and his promises. Or do you welcome the change and trust that GOD has everything under control. I watched Bishop T.D. Jakes live one time and he said that when you go through a transition period it's real rough and trying. I knew what he was saying but I didn't know that my transition would be as rough and trying as it was. Let's take Job for example, Job didn't know what was going on, all he knew was that he suddenly lost everything and his so called "friends" were accusing him of being wicked and sinning towards GOD when he knew he did no such thing. And it even got to the point where Job questioned GOD himself and was frustrated with his situation. But he never cursed GOD or never lost faith or never even questioned his power. All he wanted to know was what did he do and how could he fix it? This is a totally natural response. But when GOD answered Job, he immediately humbled himself and got back in line and apologized for questioning GOD. I wonder how many of us would do that knowing we did nothing wrong in the first place.

The bible referred to Job as "blameless", something me and you would never experience outside of Jesus. And he still had to go through, so that says a lot about GOD and how he views us. But one thing I noticed about Job was that he knew how important it was to have his heart right. The bible said that after he celebrated his children's birthdays, he would make them give a burnt sacrifice unto GOD just in case they sinned against GOD in their hearts. That is why Job qualified to go through what he went through. Now I know you are saying "qualified?" like it was a privilege for him to go through what he went through, but in actuality it was. James writes in his epistle "to count it all joy whenever trouble comes your way for your faith is tested". And later on in that same epistle he writes "GOD blesses people who patiently endure testing." And Paul writes in 2nd Corinthians about how he is content with his hardships because GOD'S favor works best when he is weak. So, you see no one suffers for nothing, the question is whether you are ready for the reward or not? Because that is what determines the end of your suffering it's all to get you ready for the next level in Christ. But sometimes GOD wants to see the fight in us; he wants to see how bad we want it. Paul wrote in the 2nd chapter of Philippians to work out your own salvation with fear and trembling. Remember slothfulness is considered a sin before GOD. So that is the fear that should fuel our fire to succeed, to go out and take what is ours. That is what Joshua's generation had to do. GOD had the promise land laid out for them but at the same time he wasn't just going to give it to them they had to fight for it, go and take it. Those actions show that you trust and believe in GOD for what he says. Saints remember this is and will always be a war and our mind state should reflect that. We should ask GOD for the mind of a soldier. Look at it this way; If you were going into battle would you take coward soldiers or strong, determined, fearless soldiers ready to fight? GOD'S answer is the same as yours. The days of crying in the face of trouble should be over. We are at war so we should expect trouble. The question is will you take an unnecessary whooping or fight back and overcome like we are commanded to do? Another thing we must realize is that it is GOD that delivers us not a job or a person. A lot of the time we'll believe GOD for something and think we know how he's going to make it happen for us and get caught up in the way we think he's going to deliver us, and our faith is directed towards the thing or person we think GOD is going to use instead of GOD himself. Don't get distracted or sidetracked, it will be GOD that brings you out, anything that happens is because GOD said so. It is easy to get caught up in such manner while going through a storm, but if we put other things before GOD we'll never get delivered. Remember we serve a jealous GOD and rightfully so. And also remember that everything is intentional. GOD is the ultimate chess player. Every move, every action that he allows has a purpose. And that purpose has your best interest in mind and heart always remember that, GOD loves you.

Reaping the Harvest

Remember when we talked about stewardship earlier in the book? That is one of the things going through a storm does for you is make you a better steward, after struggling and enduring, when you finally see better times in your life, you're reluctant to want to go back to the hard times you just came out of. So now you manage your resources much better when you come out. Another thing a storm does is make you appreciate your things even more than you did previously, therefore making you take better care of them. But keep this in mind. When it's time to reap the harvest, you should do it with your chest out. There's nothing wrong with enjoying GOD'S blessings, especially when you've earned the right to do so, through all the suffering and enduring. We should not be apologetic about prospering because it is our right to prosper; we pay the price so we should enjoy it and glorify GOD in it. Remember that saints, we endure things and times that non-believers cannot, so when it's time for the reward we well deserve it, not because we are better than anyone else, but because it has been revealed to us who is Lord and who GOD is. That is what separates us from everyone else, that is what gives us that "unfair advantage" we talked about earlier. Another thing that gives us an unfair advantage is tithing. This is a big issue in some churches if not all. There's always a couple of members that do not really get the principle of tithing. When you give that ten percent of what you make you are telling GOD that you trust him more than you trust your money and those are big words. Taking into consideration you can see your money and we see that money basically runs the world. So when you give the ten percent, it says a lot. And the money you give to your church should go towards helping the ministry to function. It's sort of like if you scratch GOD'S back, he'll scratch yours. In other words, if you pour into my kingdom, I'll pour into yours. And we all know that we cannot out-pour GOD. But all of the notions of "the preachers stealing the money" to "I'm not buying his new car" are all from the enemy. Let me ask you this. How much would you pay to keep your soul out of hell? You cannot put a price on it. So, a dime out of every dollar you make sounds like a steal if you ask me, and we are not even talking about the benefits that come with it. But there are some preachers who don't do right by GOD'S people. If your preacher or head of spiritual household is one of these people, it's your fault for staying there, you can leave whenever you get ready. If you truly in your heart do not believe the head of your spiritual household (church) is not a set man or woman of GOD you shouldn't be there. Jesus himself warned us of false prophets and said I quote "Take heed and let no man deceive you." Now I cannot blame you for not wanting to give your tithe to a thief. But it is really between you and GOD. So, you would really need to go somewhere where GOD is real, a place where you can feel his presence. But if you do feel like GOD is in your house then you have no excuse unless you are not making any money. But when Jesus said "first seek ye the kingdom of heaven" tithing is one of those actions aimed directly towards the kingdom. You cannot go wrong aiming to build up the kingdom of GOD. And tithing is not the only thing we should do when trying to build up GOD'S

Kingdom. We should also do it through our prayer. Remember we are all on the same team; every believer of Christ is together on the same team no matter what church you attend or even where you live. When we pray, we should pray for the renewal of the hearts and minds of every believer, and GOD'S hand of protection for every believer. Whatever you would ask for yourself you should ask for the body of Christ also. The goal is that we all prosper and live victoriously. Just think if 1/3 of the body of Christ prayed for the entire body of Christ how much better we would be. This would be a major step towards saving a countless number of souls. We as a body would be so strong, a force in the name of Jesus and no one could stop us from doing GOD'S will.

But when you are in the will of GOD and have made it to the place where his favor reigns in your life be careful because the enemy is going to do all he can to get you out of it. Now I'm not saying be perfect cause none of us are, but the key is to not stray away from our father, cause remember "he never leaves us we always leave him". So, if there is any separation between you and GOD you created it. If you are waiting on something from GOD keep waiting it will be well worth the wait, I promise you your actions will not be Regretted and when you do receive it be sure it is from GOD because the enemy will Camouflage himself to try to sneak in. Keep the principles of your relationship with GOD. Don't cheat on him and you can't go wrong I hope this book will help you and empower you to fight against the enemy.

Part 2

Hello, at the end of the last chapter I talked about gaining GOD'S favor and staying in GOD'S favor. Now I am going to talk about what can happen if you let the enemy trick you out of GOD'S favor. In the last chapter I showed you the way back to the garden of Eden so to speak, a place where GOD takes care of everything for you and all you must do is be obedient. But just like Adam and Eve I was tricked out of my Eden and forced to find my way back. This book is to ensure you do not make the same mistakes I have. Also, I want you to know the tricks of the enemy and how he works. So, take heed and enjoy.

Behind Enemy Lines

I've seen the power of witchcraft firsthand, and I can tell you it's no joke and also know that you really have to be rooted deeply in the word and the will of GOD to overcome it. One thing I learned is that it's not that their god is greater than ours it's the fact that they are more committed to their god than we are to ours. Understand that these people dedicate their life to sin and being deceitful. And pleasing their god while we are reducing our Father to a Sunday morning affair and straddling the fence on whether we want to please him or ourselves first. Don't get me wrong I know it's easier just to do wrong and live selfishly, but it's also easy to believe that GOD is the great I am and also that he loves us more than we love ourselves, also GOD knows us better than we know ourselves because he created us. I'm saying that to say this. WE DO NOT HAVE TO BE PERFECT TO COME TO GOD. Because we are not able to make ourselves perfect. I think there is a notion as believers that we must be "Holy" before we can pray to GOD or even come to him. GOD loves you pass your faults and struggles. GOD wants to take those from you. But you have to be willing to come to him and give them up so it can happen. Don't let doubt and shame keep away from GOD. Doubt and shame are tools of the enemy. And speaking of the enemy. If you pay attention to the level of dedication they show to the enemy, you'll realize that we are bringing a knife to a gun fight when we have the bigger guns at home, now how dumb is that? For example, they hold spiritual rituals where they sacrifice animals to get their god's attention, and to get him to show his power. But what do we do outside of say a little weak prayer that we halfway believe and then turn right around and offend him. Now I'm not saying go and start sacrificing animals. But we can start sacrificing our sins. Take Jesus for example, remember he performed all of his miracles through faith and not as the son of GOD but as the son of man. That is why he said we will do more than what he did. But the point I'm trying to make is this, Jesus didn't have a part-time relationship with the father, his entire being was dedicated to the will of GOD. That's where the close relationship, unparalleled level of faith, and power came from. The answers you need and the life that GOD wants us to live are all in the bible. We as Christians have a tremendous opportunity at life, but we must handle this life the way GOD wants us to handle it. GOD is the creator of all, and the bible are instructions straight from him on what he expects from us. How well will you follow instructions?

The reason I went through storms is because I compromised my relationship with GOD for one night it led to the roughest year of my life. I found myself in a situation where witchcraft and idolatry were all around me being practiced like it was normal and most of all, they tried to make it look like it was tied to Jesus by quoting scriptures while praying to idol gods. I knew that was wrong and not what GOD intended. I found myself in shops where they sold false idols and other items of witchcraft, saints let me tell you this stuff is real and not to be played with if your faith is not strong. I also found myself living with a demon who's only purpose was to destroy me. This spirit was so twisted and it seemed could take on so many forms to manipulate whoever came across it's path, it really gave me an in-depth look at the enemy and how he works. First off let me start off by saying when the bible says "the devil is a liar and there is no truth in him" that's exactly what it means this demon lied about everything small stuff to big it got to the point where I couldn't believe anything I was hearing because nothing was true anymore. Also, I can say that demons are absolutely positively afraid of praise when it is sincere and from the heart. Demons cannot stand to be around they have to leave cause the presence of GOD is coming there were numerous times where I turned on the television and a powerful song of praise comes on and the demon would run out of the room. At the time I did not notice what was going on but now when I look back over the situation, I can remember a couple of things that should've let me know what I was dealing with. To be honest GOD showed me in a dream what I was getting into as a warning sign to get out and leave but I ignored it. I can remember the dream like it was yesterday. I was in the apartment that she lived in and she was laying in the bed with her back towards me and when I went to touch her she immediately jumped up and her face was that of a demon. Eyes and tongue like a snake and hair like Medusa it was standing up on her head and waving around like a snake. I knew when I woke up it was GOD showing me the spirit of this woman and telling me what I was doing but the enemy immediately came and blamed himself for the dream. It was crazy how the enemy wanted me to believe it was him playing a trick on me so I would stay in the situation. That showed me that the enemy would stop at nothing to destroy one of us. The under-handed thinking I've witnessed from the enemy showed me that the enemy is always thinking and always thinking a couple steps ahead. I told you earlier that the enemy has a plan just like GOD does. But thanks to Jesus the Christ GOD has the final say so over what happens to us. Cause if not be for the blood of Jesus I would have died in hurricane Katrina even though I live in Memphis. Let me explain. The demon wanted to take me to New Orleans for my birthday which was during the week, so we decided to go that weekend the same weekend Katrina came. Our plan was to leave a full day before the storm was supposed to hit, so the last night we were there we go on Bourbon street and on the way back an argument started and she walks off and leaves me while I'm using the bathroom, so I'm lost on Bourbon street and had to find my way back to the hotel we were staying at. To make a long story short the demon physically starts a fight and calls the police to try to have me arrested knowing there's a storm coming. If I'm in jail, there's no way I can go back home and I'm dead when the storm hits. But GOD stepped in and made sure I made it out alright. Saints the bible is true the enemy wants to kill you but only by the grace and mercy of GOD our Father he is not allowed to because he does not have that authority.

The authority lies within us as believers, we decide what we will and what we will not allow the enemy to do in our lives. I chose to ignore the signs GOD gave me and paid dearly for it. I made the mistake of thinking I can save everybody, and the truth is beloved that we cannot save everybody. "GOD made the wicked for hell" said Soloman in Proverbs, and that is something we have to come to grips with. If you meet someone that is wicked, you have to shake the dust off of your feet and keep moving or they'll try their best to bring you down, it is their job to do so. Just like it is our job to save souls it's their job to corrupt them and they will corrupt yours if surround yourself with them.

Do not let the enemy use your religion against you. Also respect your weakness, none of us are perfect. Know this and keep this in mind because the enemy will use your weakness to get you out of the favor of GOD. Witches and Warlocks do exist and some of them even come to church so we must be incredibly careful who we get involved with as believers. Some of the things to look for are manipulative spirits; people who manipulate other people for their own gain, also a rebellious spirit; someone who will try to force their will upon a situation instead of letting the will of GOD be done. Also, heavy drinking is another one to watch out for, you notice that some liquor stores refer to their products as "spirits" that is not an coincidence they are called that for a reason. That is why we must stay in the word of GOD because it tells us what to look for and how to spot these spirits. For example, the bible says "let everything that hath breath praise ye the Lord" if you see someone sitting in a worship service where the spirit and praise is high and they either leave or sit there with their arms folded that is something to keep your eye on. Paul writes about these same signs in Galatians the 5th chapter 19th verse other signs he name are such as sexual immorality, impure thoughts, eagerness for lustful pleasure, participation in demonic activities, hostility, quarreling, jealousy, outburst of anger, selfish ambition, the feeling that everyone is wrong except those in their own little group, envy, and wild parties.

I speak this from knowledge of the situation. I hear people say all the time that "only if Adam hadn't eaten that fruit, we would be better off". Not true, all the generations of people between us and Adam and you think nobody would have ate from the tree in all of that time? It was bound to happen. It is not the fact that they ate from the tree, it is the fact that they, just like all of us have a weakness as people we all have a weakness the enemy played on their weakness and has played on ours many of times. So I know you're probably saying something like, "I wasn't in paradise either". Well, were you? Have you been in a situation so good you could not believe it? It was like nothing could go wrong in your life. What happened to the situation and why are you not in it anymore? Is it because you did something to offend GOD? And if so then you are no different from Adam or Eve.

If we can understand where GOD is coming from maybe, we can understand why we go through the things we go through. Keep in mind that GOD operates on a much higher level than we do. Look at the love he displayed for us. He came down himself and died for us. And not a quick death either. He suffered a great deal; he was tortured for at least a day or two and even lay dead for three days. He did this not for himself because he was good where he was with no risk of going to hell. He did not need Calvary one bit. But he did what he did for us so we would not be lost forever. I can say that nobody we know, or love would go through that for us..." nobody". So, when we hurt GOD you have to imagine the pain and the hurt that he feels. So maybe just maybe that is why he allows us to suffer right to the point of breaking down and giving up, to give us a taste of how he feels when we hurt him. Think about it.

Also think about this, the fact that you have confessed Jesus the Christ as LORD and savior. So, with that comes a higher standard, people and GOD will hold you to a higher standard. Things "normal" people do should not be the things you do. Things "normal" people say should not be the things you say. The way "normal" people think should not be the way you think. You ever noticed the double standard when dealing with unsaved or non- believing people. It's like bad rude and ill-mannered behavior is cool for them but let a Christian slip up and their whole faith is challenged or questioned. That is because we are held to a higher standard than other people because we have a higher power in our corner and living in us. So therefore, we should know better. That's what the unsaved people are saying, and you know what, they are right. GOD wants us to be held to a higher standard and also to uphold that standard because it's a testimony to him and his goodness. But one bad decision, one bad mistake can erase all your good deeds in the eyes of those who watch you when you confess JESUS as Lord. At the end of the day, we are not perfect and will make mistakes, but it is how we handle the mistake is the most important thing, the non-believer needs to know that GOD is forgiving and is willing to keep fighting for us as. So, we must be extra careful in how we live saints. Because a lot is riding on our behavior. A lot of souls hang in the balance and a bad example can sway them the wrong way. So, therefore GOD allows us to be held to a higher standard. Because we are called to live life on a higher level than people who do not know JESUS. But this does not go unrewarded, GOD will also prosper you so that the people who watch you can see what living according to GOD's will, can and will eventually take them. The reward is greater for the one who works the hardest and is more dedicated. This principle applies in both your spiritual and physical walk. Remember the more GOD can trust you with, the more he can give you. So, show GOD that you can handle wealth and prosperity and not let it corrupt you. Instead show GOD that you will be a blessing to him and to everyone else you come in contact with. That is how we will save souls and show people the true goodness of GOD. That is how we will be light among the darkness and be more like our Lord and savior Jesus the Christ.

Faith

Let's talk about faith for a minute. We as Christians need to understand just how important it is to our relationship GOD. The bible says without faith it is impossible to please GOD. Hebrews the 11th chapter talks about faith and says it is the "confident assurance that what we hope for is going to happen". I will take it farther than that, I'll say "it is the confident assurance that what we hope for and more will happen." We all know that GOD is the GOD of abundance and always gives us more than we need. Faith is the single thing that determines where your relationship with GOD is headed. The more you trust him the more he trusts you the more he trusts you means the higher he can take you in him. And also, the more you trust him the more like him you become. And that is the whole purpose of it all, to become more like him. If you look at most prominent, powerful, and prosperous people in the world you will notice that their way of thinking is different from people who are not as prominent or prosperous. It is like they are thinking on a higher level. Because they are. GOD has seen a lot of himself in these people and trust them with a lot more because he knows they can handle the responsibility. Now let me clarify the last statement. I'm not calling anybody "holier than thou", what I mean when I say this is that God sees a lot of himself as far as being a steward in these people. The ability to manage so to speak, and that is what

I mean when I say, "sees a lot of himself". Remember Jesus did his miracles by faith. He has a level of trust with GOD like no other. He literally trusted GOD enough to lay down his life and look how he turned out. But how do we get faith? By enduring through trials and tribulation.

It is there where our faith is tested and either made stronger or is lost, let me explain. When I say "is made stronger" I mean you can choose to hold on through the tough times and continue to believe in GOD for your victory. GOD will always bring you out that is why it is important that you trust him for your own good cause you will gain in the end. The harder the trial and tribulation the greater the reward because you have displayed more trust for him. Now when I say "is lost" I mean you can simply give up on GOD and go back to your old way of thinking and do some things that are not exactly pleasing to GOD. Paul writes in Romans 8:18(NLT) That what we suffer now is nothing compared to the glory he will give us later. Let us take Jesus for example, you probably won't hear anybody else say this but "Jesus got over". Let me explain. Keep romans 8:18 in mind. And I will show you how true it is. Jesus was beaten and killed for a crime he did not commit, laid dead for three days where he went to hell for our sins and redeemed us. Now after all that he ends up with infinite power and eternal reign! Is that a sweet deal or what?! I know what you are thinking. "Yeah, but none of us could endure what Jesus went through." And you are right, none of us could. But he could because of the level of trust he has in the Father. This is the same man who walked on water when GOD asked him to. I mean how many of us would do that? The point I'm trying to make is this. If you trust GOD through whatever your trial or tribulation may be, you will have a sweet deal too. Remember to trust and believe in GOD because he will always bring you out.

Paul wrote in Romans 4; 27-28 that "our acquittal is not based on our good deeds. It is based on our faith. So, we are made right with GOD through our faith and not by obeying the law. Paul is basically saying that faith has the power to redeem mankind from any transgressions towards GOD. That is a powerful statement but a true one, it's through our faith in JESUS the Christ that we are able to repent and come to GOD through prayer even though he views us as "filthy rags". Paul also talks about Abraham and how he was declared righteous through his faith not his work. In other words, Abraham did nothing to merit GOD accepting him. He received the promise by faith in GOD, and he also compares faith to a circumcision, which is defined as the removal of excess flesh. Well faith does this in a way, the more faith you have the less you give in to the will of your flesh. And therefore, you will walk after your spirit more and more. But this is not as easy as it sounds because GOD will ask you to believe him in some tough situations. But keep in mind that GOD has a plan for you and would not ask you to do anything that does not have purpose. It is to build "character" as Paul calls it and prepare you for you work in Christ.

Prayer

The word prayer in the Webster's dictionary is defined as a "a humble request to GOD." "An entreaty; supplication. the key word in that definition was humble, keep in mind that this is an almighty GOD who could destroy you and send you to hell. He knows it, you know it and he should be treated as such. With that being said, don't be too afraid to ask for what you really want, just make sure that it lines up with his word. Now the bible defines the word prayer as a conversation with GOD in praise, thanksgiving, or intercession. Both of these are true, Prayer can be used for either one of these purposes. That is why we as believers need to grasp the true concept of prayer. Let us take the Lord's prayer for example, Jesus asked for daily bread, forgiveness for others, and the will of GOD to be done. These things should be included in all our prayers. But one thing I also noticed was even Jesus humbled himself before asking for any of these things, he started his prayer off with praise acknowledging GOD for who he is first. Paul wrote in Hebrews that whoever comes to GOD must believe that there is a GOD and is a rewarder of those who sincerely seek him. Do you sincerely seek him? Or do you only seek him when you need him? GOD answers prayer but GOD does not want to have to dump trouble on you all the time just to get your attention either. So, it is great when you can just come to GOD just to give him praise and thanksgiving, even if things are not going your way GOD still is good and deserves the praise, it is not good to come to GOD with your hand out all the time.

Jesus spoke about prayer in the 21st chapter of Matthew he said in Matt. 21: 21-22 (NLT) that "if you have faith and don't doubt you can do things like this and much more. You can even say to this mountain, 'May GOD lift you up and throw you into the sea, 'and it will happen. If you believe you will receive whatever you ask for in prayer." This scripture is a confirmation that doubt is a tool of the enemy that is used to hinder our authority and growth as believers. I spoke earlier about how we should treat fear, as a green light as a sign to let you know you are on the right path. Doubt should be treated the same way. You see everything I have shared with you in this book has to come together in your prayer life, with faith being the most important. Also, one thing I want to talk about is the blood of our Lord and savior Jesus the Christ. This is a powerful weapon that can be used in prayer you see; the blood of Jesus is what redeemed all mankind from sin and defeated the enemy and it gives us the authority that we have over him. The blood of Jesus can be used as protection from the enemy by declaring that our savior's blood is against him and that he cannot stand, remember every knee shall bow and every tongue shall confess that Jesus is Lord even the enemy's knee will bow, and he knows this, but we must let him know that we know this as well. Saints understand that the very authority that was left behind for us by our Lord and Savior lies in his blood and our belief in him.

An important key in prayer is asking for what you want, be specific. James writes in the 4th chapter of his epistle that you have not cause you ask not. Now this is not a green light to go and ask GOD for a million dollars if you are not willing to put in the work or go through the necessary tests. He also writes in the 5th chapter that the earnest prayer of a righteous person has great power and wonderful results. The word earnest is defined as serious, intense, in a determined manner. So, the key is to be determined, specific, and have no doubt. Prayer is an effective weapon in battles with witchcraft and other demonic forces also but again, we have to be specific in what we ask for, we must single out what we believe that it is we are up against whether it be the spirit of witchcraft or a demonic spirit we have to go to GOD about that spirit in particular in order to be effective in rebuking that spirit in the name of JESUS. Another effective weapon is fasting, Jesus states in Matthew 17:21 that certain demons can only be driven out by fasting and prayer, this coupled with an undoubted belief in GOD is unstoppable and will be highly effective in battling the enemy. I go on a 24 hour fast once a week and I noticed that my spirit got stronger with each one, fasting to me is like "a spiritual weight room". Fasting weakens the desires of the flesh and forces you to go strictly on your spirit. It is a rough thing to endure but the rewards are well worth it, spiritual strength and a guaranteed response from GOD you cannot beat that. Next time you are in need of something trying fasting and prayer and watch the difference. The word fast is defined as; to abstain from all or certain foods. So, this means you can give up everything or just certain things for a certain amount of time the choice is yours, but I would advise anyone to work their way up to a 24 hour no food or liquids fast, start at 8-12 hours and work your way up. But this is something we as believers must do in our relationship with GOD. And we can do it just because not only when we are in need but as a token of love to our father.

Marriage

The enemy is attacking marriages left and right, but GOD shared a particularly important key with me that I'm going to share with you, that key is communication. Communication is very key in any relationship; it is important that husband and wife know what each other is thinking and what direction each individual sees and wants the marriage to go. Mark 10: 6-9 says that a man and wife are as one. It also talks about how a man should leave mother and father and cling to his wife, for they are no longer two but one. That means you two should move and think as one. James wrote in his epistle that a double minded man is unstable in all his ways. This will apply to a double minded marriage as well, the two must come together and compromise and agree on everything as one person not two. Jesus also said, "wherever two or more gather in my name touching and agreeing there I will be in the midst". But the two parties must have an open mind about this and be willing to admit when they are wrong and that the other person's idea may be better than theirs sometimes, being humble towards your spouse is not a bad thing. It is the right thing because you two are a gift from GOD to each other. And remember what Jesus said in Mark 3:25 "A house divided against itself is doomed." Therefore, the King and queen should stand united on everything. Now I understand that we as people will not agree on everything but that's where compromising comes in. Find a happy medium that both people can live with. This is something me and my wife learned the hard way. We would be at odds with each other and instead of talking about the situation in a calm and sensible manner. We would just hold it in and try to deal with it within ourselves. Listen to how crazy that sounds, we would try to fix a problem that we had with one another by not talking to each other. Needless to say, that did not work out well at all. But once we started to talk about our feelings towards each other and the situations that we faced the problems seemed to vanish after we would talk about it, but this was because we came to a mutual understanding about the situation and made a compromise or a decision to agree to disagree on some things. And also, we have to develop is a sense of security that when you and your spouse took your vows that you both absolutely meant them. In other words, you two should be able to talk to each other about anything and I do mean anything. My wife and I even talk to each other about which celebrities we think are the most attractive. Because we know that no matter how attractive the next person is you can only have one soul mate. and we believe that we have found ours in each other. Me and my wife had a few situations that were caused by a lack of communication that also caused a void in our relationship emotionally. Both of us had always been loners and always dealt with emotional issues within ourselves, and we brought those same behaviors into our marriage, but we learned that a lot of the things you did while being single, and a lot of the ways you operate can't and won't work when there are two people involved. We also had to learn to share our true feelings no matter how it may affect the other person. This can also lead to a stronger bond emotionally and a stronger emotional bond will benefit all areas of the marriage, and men I do mean all areas. Sex is a very emotional act to a woman and if she is not connected to you emotionally it will not be as good for you two as it can be. She must feel like you will be there for her in all areas as a best friend would, matter of fact you should be her best friend and vice versa. That is an important need for a woman and man alike, friendship should be the foundation for any marriage. Wives should be willing to watch football with their husbands and guys we should make some sacrifices too and do things with our spouse that we do not necessarily like to do. Now back to sex, the bible speaks on sex, Hebrews 13:4 says that "the bed is undefiled to a married couple". I do not know about you, but to me that sounds like anything goes if you are married. So, with that being said, talk to your spouse about sex. Also, we talked about earlier to share your true feelings. Because your mate must know what you like and how you like it and who knows better than you.

Another important principle in communicating is establishing a "chain of command". Let me explain, your boss at work has a boss that he or she reports to and so on and so on until you get to the top. we should have the same chain of command in our households. Men the bible says that we are like Christ in our marriage in other words, we are supposed to minister the word of GOD to our houses. The direction of your household depends on you and your relationship with GOD. The chain of command should be GOD talking to the man (head) of the house and he should pass the direction on to the rest of the house. This is the same order GOD had with Moses when he led his people out of Egypt, and the same order he had with Adam and Eve in the beginning. But notice how head was written in parenthesis, that was done for a reason. Because the man is not always the head of the house, either the man is absent physically or spiritually. GOD will speak to the one who is closest to him. And a lot of the times it is the wife and not the husband. Now men this should not be. As the King we must realize that everything that happens in our kingdom is directly tied to the decisions that we made. Money has nothing to do with who is considered to be the head of the house, it's about whom is more mature spiritually and who is more fit to lead. Because that person is more inclined to hearing GOD and establishing GOD's order within the household. Men that should be us it is what GOD had intended for us from the beginning. But thank GOD for a wife who can pick up the slack until we can get ourselves in line with the will of GOD because without them the marriage will fail. Men we must get closer to GOD and ask him for direction, that we may give direction to the rest of the household. Now in the book of Genesis it talks about the first marriage ever, Adam and Eve. Notice how GOD established the law with Adam and trusted him to relay it to Eve. But when the law was not upheld GOD addressed Adam first because he was supposed to uphold the law. Likewise, with men in our households, imagine how better off we would be with more strong men in the houses upholding the values of GOD. This is the type of structure that GOD intended for us as his people. Now on the flip side of that when Adam disobeyed GOD his punishment spread abroad unto every living thing on earth. Paul wrote in Romans the 5th chapter that when Adam sinned, sin entered the entire human race. Adam's sin brough death, so death spread to everyone, for everyone sinned.

There is a saying that the blessings flow through the head of the household but also curses and death can flow through the head of the household too. So, men we must be extra careful what we partake in and how we stand with GOD. Because it is more than just your life that will be affected by your actions. Also, men we need to be very aware of how we treat our wives as well. The bible says that he who finds a wife finds a good thing.

The bible also refers to the wife as a perfect gift from GOD. And he must be pleased with the way you treat your wife as well as your possessions. You are responsible for everything in your house as the head of your house. Also, men it is imperative that we walk in the will of GOD and that is more than just reading the word it is living it also. I challenge you to actively seek GOD and ask him what is your role in his kingdom? Once you commit your life to that, you cannot lose. Being obedient to the will of GOD and living the life he calls us to live. Sacrificing whatever GOD tells us too. This will make us effective leaders not only in our home but outside of the home as well, because at this point you are being led by GOD himself that is the unfair advantage that I spoke of earlier.

The Mirror

The reason this chapter is named "the mirror" is because that is where true self-improvement lies. It is when we can look at ourselves and be 100% truthful in what we see in ourselves. What we do well and most importantly what we do wrong. Once we come to the realization that we are not perfect and that we can always improve and also, it's ok to have flaws. Then we can truly improve ourselves and our relationship with GOD, and relationships with everyone else in our lives. That is why it is important to stay humble. A prideful and vain person cannot truly evaluate themselves because their insecurities will not allow them to see their own flaws. This is a tricky thing because you must remain humble and confident at the same time, let me explain, and you will see that the two actually go hand in hand. When you are humble you realize that you have no ability and the ability that you are confident in is the ability of GOD himself. You must fully submit yourself to the will of GOD. Now to those of you who would say" I thought Paul wrote in the new testament to work out your own salvation?" I say this to you, the way to do that is to submit to GOD's plan, remember GOD has a purpose for each and every one of us before we were formed in our mother's womb. The way to work out your own salvation is to find this purpose and fulfill it. The process of going to the mirror is a never-ending thing also, Isaiah speaks of teaching knowledge in the 28th chapter and explains the process as line being upon line and precept being upon precept. He never speaks of an end and if we are to be in Christ who himself is in GOD the father who has no end to his wisdom and power therefore the improvement process should be and never ending one as well.

Another step to this process is knowing what it is that you are looking at when you are looking in the mirror, to selfevaluate. Know that whatever truth that you see whatever is keeping you from evolving as a person is there for one reason and one reason only and that is to destroy you and rob you of joy, prosperity, and peace of mind also is it there to hinder your relationship with GOD. So, in other words we must identify our sin and get rid of it. Sin has the power to totally destroy not only our relationship with GOD, but our very lives also. The book of Enoch is a book that is not in the regular King James Bible it is a separate book, and in this book, it talks about how angels sinned against GOD by descending to earth to mate with humans. This sin angered GOD so much that he cast the angels out of heaven to a place where they asked Enoch a mere mortal, a human to go to GOD and make intercession for them to ask for forgiveness. Now think about that for a minute. These were almighty angels with the power to destroy the earth, and sin reduced them to a state to where they could not even go to GOD for themselves. Sin and disobedience are tools of the devil and they WILL destroy us if we do not identify them a eliminate them. The bible states that the wages of sin are death because all sin will eventually lead you there. Think about it, when you look at the murder mystery shows the murder victim almost always has some sin that he or she is committing that ultimately lead to his or her death. But it is not just a physical death that we have to be aware of, death can come in many forms whether it be spiritually, mentally, or emotional. Death can also come to certain things in your life such as your job or your marriage. So, when the scripture says the wages of sin is death it is not always a physical one.

Declaration

GOD, my father and my everything. I want to declare that without you in my life father I would be nothing. A homeless man on the streets or somewhere dead or locked up. You saved me so many times, and gave me so many chances it is ridiculous, and father I can't thank you enough I can work for an eternity and still owe you for all you've done. You are Alpha and Omega, the almighty Supreme Being with infinite wisdom and power. And I thank you for trusting me with the knowledge you have shared with me. I pray in the name of Jesus that this book brings the body of Christ to a whole new level in you, and ultimately brings us closer to you. And will also make us more pleasing to you father, Amen.

My Thanks

I want to thank all of you for reading GOD'S word and supporting me in my service to our Father. I pray that this book brings you closer to GOD than you have ever been. I pray that your spirit will grow by leaps and bounds so that you may fully experience the goodness of God our Father, and save some souls along the way, that your living will not be in vain. And last but certainly not least I want to thank my beautiful wife who stood by me and supported me through all the tough times you just read about. And if not for her and GOD I would not have made it through them. May the peace, blessings, and most of all power of GOD our Father be with you in your daily living. These things I declare in your life in the name of Jesus. Amen (1 John 2:17 And the world is passing away, and the lust of it; but he who does the will of GOD abides forever.) Will you abide forever?